Basic
social skills
for youth

D1540508

$5.12

Also from the Boys Town Press

BOOKS

Teaching Social Skills to Youth
Boundaries: A Guide for Teens
A Good Friend
Who's in the Mirror?
What's Right for Me?
The Well-Managed Classroom
Getting Along With Others: Activity Book
Common Sense Parenting®
Unmasking Sexual Con Games: Student Guide
La Crianza Práctica de los Hijos
Practical Tools for Foster Parents
Safe and Effective Secondary Schools
Parenting to Build Character in Your Teen
Common Sense Parenting of Toddlers and Preschoolers
The Ongoing Journey: Awakening Spiritual Life in At-Risk Youth
Working with Aggressive Youth
Building Skills in High-Risk Families: Strategies for the Home-Based Practitioner
Rebuilding Children's Lives: A Blueprint for Treatment Foster Parents
Effective Skills for Child-Care Workers
Caring for Youth in Shelters
Time to Enrich K-6 and 7-12 Activity Kits

VIDEO

Common Sense Parenting®: Helping Your Child Succeed
Common Sense Parenting®: Teaching Responsible Behavior
Videos for Parents Series
Sign With Me: A Family Sign Language Curriculum Series
Read With Me: Storytelling with Deaf Toddlers

AUDIO

One to One: Personal Counseling Tapes for Teens
Common Sense Parenting®

For a free copy of the Boys Town Press catalog, call **1-800-282-6657**
www.girlsandboystown.org/btpress

Basic social skills for youth

A handbook from Boys Town

BOYS TOWN PRESS

BOYS TOWN, NEBRASKA

Basic social skills for youth

Published by The Boys Town Press
Father Flanagan's Boys' Home
Boys Town, Nebraska 68010

ISBN 0-938510-39-8

The Boys Town Press is the publishing division of Girls and Boys Town, the original Father Flanagan's Boys' Home.

20   19   18   17   16   15   14   13   12   11

Basic skill 3

Talking with others

Not a day goes by that you don't talk to someone. Knowing how to engage in a conversation makes the experience pleasurable for both you and the other person. People are more likely to want to talk to you and listen to what you have to say when you know how to participate in a conversation. Follow these steps whether you're talking to a friend, a teacher, or someone you just met. Engaging in a conversation is a skill that everyone needs.

Step 1. Look at the person.

Step 2. Use a pleasant voice.

Step 3. Ask questions.

Step 4. Don't interrupt.

Talking with others

Step 1. Look at the person.

Rationale:

Looking at the person shows that you are paying attention and shows the person that you want to talk.

Helpful hints:

- Look at the person as you would a friend.
- Look at the person's face; this will help you understand that person's mood.

Step 2. Use a pleasant voice.

Rationale:

People won't want to talk to someone who seems unpleasant, angry, or threatening.

Helpful hints:

- Speak clearly.
- Use short sentences that are easily understood.
- Think before you speak.

Step 3. Ask questions.

Rationale:

Asking questions includes the other person in the conversation.

Helpful hints:

- Avoid asking questions that can be answered with a "Yes" or a "No."

- Ask the person about his or her opinions, likes and dislikes, and interests. Share your opinions as well.

- Listen intently.

- Be prepared to answer questions the person might ask you.

Step 4. Don't interrupt.

Rationale:

Interrupting shows you don't care what the other person is saying.

Helpful hints:

- Make sure the person is done speaking before you respond.

- Maintain eye contact.

- Maintain good posture; don't distract the other person by yawning or looking bored.

- Don't monopolize the conversation or jump from topic to topic.

Basic skill 4

Introducing yourself

The first time you meet someone usually gives you an idea of what kind of person he or she is. That is why it is so important for you to learn how to greet others. First impressions are lasting impressions. By following the steps for greeting others, you show that you are friendly and really interested in meeting new people. Follow the same steps in any situation where you are meeting someone for the first time. You'll feel more comfortable and relaxed, and so will the other person.

Step 1. Look at the person. Smile.

Step 2. Use a pleasant voice.

Step 3. Offer a greeting. Say "Hi, my name is..."

Step 4. Shake the person's hand.

Step 5. When you leave, say "It was nice to meet you."

Introducing yourself

Step 1. Look at the person.

Rationale:

Looking at the person is one way of showing that you really want to meet him or her.

Helpful hints:

- Get the person's attention appropriately.
- Don't stare or make faces.
- Look at the person as you would a friend.
- Looking at the person sets a friendly tone for the beginning of your conversation.

Step 2. Use a pleasant voice.

Rationale:

You will make a good impression if you appear to be friendly.

Helpful hints:

- Speak clearly.
- Talk loud enough to be heard, but not too loud.
- Use proper grammar and avoid slang words.
- Don't interrupt.

Step 3. Say "Hi, my name is..."

<u>Rationale:</u>

Saying "Hi" shows you are friendly and makes the other person feel welcome.

<u>Helpful hints:</u>

- Make sure the person hears you.
- Listen if the other person says anything in return.
- Smile if it is appropriate to do so.

Step 4. Shake the person's hand.

<u>Rationale:</u>

Shaking hands is a traditional way of greeting someone.

<u>Helpful hints:</u>

- Use a firm grip, but don't squeeze too hard.
- Three shakes is about right when shaking hands.
- Say "It's nice to meet you" as you shake hands.
- Make sure your hand is clean before shaking hands with someone.

Step 5. When you leave, say "It was nice to meet you."

<u>Rationale:</u>

Saying something nice ends your conversation on a friendly note.

<u>Helpful hints:</u>

- Be sincere.
- Use the person's name again when saying good-bye.
- Remember the person's name should you meet again.

Basic skill 5

Accepting criticism or a consequence

Everyone makes mistakes. We all have to deal with criticism from time to time. For example, teachers will have to correct your mistakes on tests and reports in school. Being able to accept criticism shows that you are willing to learn from your mistakes. When you can accept criticism calmly, people are going to be more likely to praise you when you do a good job. They will see that you are a person who doesn't get angry over mistakes. This will help you get along better with others.

Step 1. Look at the person.

Step 2. Say "Okay."

Step 3. Don't argue.

Accepting criticism or a consequence

Step 1. Look at the person.

Rationale:

Looking at the person shows that you are paying attention.

Helpful hints:

- Don't stare or make faces.

- Look at the person throughout the conversation. Don't look away.

- Listen carefully and try not to be distracted.

- Paying attention shows courtesy; looking away shows disinterest.

Step 2. Say "Okay."

Rationale:

Saying "Okay" shows that you understand what the other person is saying.

Helpful hints:

- Nodding your head also shows that you understand.

- Don't mumble.

- By nodding your head or saying "Okay" frequently throughout a long conversation, you let the speaker know that you are still listening carefully.

- Use a pleasant tone of voice. Don't be sarcastic.

Step 3. Don't argue.

<u>Rationale:</u>

Accepting criticism without arguing shows that you are mature.

<u>Helpful hints:</u>

- Stay calm.

- Try to learn from what the person is saying so you can do a better job next time.

- Remember that the person who is giving you criticism is only trying to help.

- If you disagree, wait until later to discuss the matter.

Basic skill 6

Disagreeing appropriately

Some people might think that if two people disagree, they have to argue or fight. That's not true. By learning how to disagree appropriately, you can avoid arguments and unpleasant situations that can arise when people don't see eye to eye. It's important to express your opinion when you disagree. Following these steps allows you to do that calmly and clearly. Your opinion will be taken more seriously when you learn and use this valuable skill.

Step 1. Look at the person.

Step 2. Use a pleasant voice.

Step 3. Say "I understand how you feel."

Step 4. Tell why you feel differently.

Step 5. Give a reason

Step 6. Listen to the other person

Disagreeing appropriately

Step 1. Look at the person.

Rationale:

Looking at the person shows that you are paying attention.

Helpful hints:

- Don't stare or make faces.
- Keep looking at the person throughout your conversation.
- Be pleasant and smile.
- Look at the person as you would a friend.

Step 2. Use a pleasant voice.

Rationale:

The person is more likely to listen to you if you use a pleasant voice.

Helpful hints:

- Speak slowly and clearly. Don't mumble.
- Use short sentences. They are easily understood.
- Keep a comfortable distance between you and the other person while you are talking.
- Smile. People are more comfortable talking with someone who is friendly.

Step 3. Say "I understand how you feel."

Rationale:

Saying you understand gets the conversation off to a positive start.

Helpful hints:

- Plan what you are going to say before you start to speak.

- If you still feel uneasy about how you are going to start your conversation, practice.

- Start to discuss your concerns as part of a conversation, not a confrontation.

- Be sincere.

Step 4. Tell why you feel differently.

Rationale:

Using vague words can lead to confusion and doesn't get your point across.

Helpful hints:

- Use as much detailed information as possible.

- Be prepared to back up what you say.

- If necessary, practice what you are going to say.

- Always remember to think before you speak.

Step 5. Give a reason.

Rationale:

Your disagreement will carry more weight if you give a valid reason.

Helpful hints:

- Be sure that your reasons make sense.
- Support your reasons with facts and details.
- One or two reasons are usually enough.
- Remember to stay calm during the conversation.

Step 6. Listen to the other person

Rationale:

Listening shows you respect what the other person has to say.

Helpful hints:

- Don't look away or make faces while the other person is talking.
- Don't interrupt.
- Stay calm.
- Don"t argue.

Basic skill 7

Showing respect

If you expect other people to respect you and your property, you have to do the same for them. When you show respect, other people see you as a kind, considerate, caring person. You will enjoy being around people and they will enjoy being around you. People are more willing to accept and like you because you know how to act appropriately in public. Getting along with others will make you feel good about yourself. Following the steps outlined here also can help you stay out of trouble.

Showing respect wherever you are:

Step 1. Obey a request to stop a negative behavior.

Step 2. Refrain from teasing, threatening, or making fun of others.

Step 3. Allow others to have their privacy.

Step 4. Obtain permission before using another person's property.

Showing respect in public:

Step 1. Do not damage or vandalize public property.

Step 2. Refrain from conning or persuading others into breaking rules.

Step 3. Avoid acting obnoxiously in public.

Step 4. Dress appropriately in public.

Showing respect

Showing respect wherever you are:

Step 1. Obey a request to stop a negative behavior.

Rationale:

When you obey a request to stop a negative behavior, you show that you can follow instructions. Being able to follow instructions is one form of showing respect.

Helpful hints:

- By stopping your negative behavior, you may avoid getting into trouble.

- There will always be people who have authority over you. You must do what they say.

Step 2. Refrain from teasing, threatening, or making fun of others.

Rationale:

By refraining from such behaviors, it shows you understand that teasing, threatening, and making fun can be hurtful to others.

Helpful hints:

- If you are always making fun of people or threatening them, you won't have many friends.

- People will think of you only as a tease, not as a nice person.

Step 3. Allow others to have their privacy.

<u>Rationale:</u>

Sometimes people need or want to be alone. You show respect by adhering to their wishes.

<u>Helpful</u> <u>hints:</u>

- Always knock before entering someone's room or a room with a closed door.

- Honor someone's desire to be left alone.

Step 4. Obtain permission before using another person's property.

<u>Rationale:</u>

You have certain possessions that are very important to you. You don't want people using them without permission. When you ask permission to use others' things, you show that same kind of respect.

<u>Helpful</u> <u>hints:</u>

- Always return items in the same condition as when you borrowed them.

- If you damage a borrowed item, offer to repair or replace it.

Showing respect in public:

Step 1. Do not damage or vandalize public property.

Rationale:

Vandalism and damaging property are against the law. Besides getting into trouble, you show disrespect for your community and country when you vandalize public property.

Helpful hints:

- Accidents do happen, but they always should be reported.

- Offer to replace or repair property you have damaged.

Step 2. Refrain from conning or persuading others into breaking rules.

Rationale:

People will think less of you if you are always trying to take advantage of others or get them into trouble.

Helpful hints:

- If you use people, they won't trust you.

- People don't appreciate being manipulated.

Step 3. Avoid acting obnoxiously in public.

Rationale:

You make a good impression with people when you show that you know how to behave and use proper social skills in public.

Helpful hints:

- Be on your best behavior in public. That means don't do such things as curse, swear, spit, or belch.

- Be courteous to others and mind your manners.

Step 4. Dress appropriately when in public.

Rationale:

When in public, people are expected to look their best. When you live up to this expectation, you show that you are mature and understand society's rules.

Helpful hints:

- Being well-groomed and well-dressed makes a good impression.

- Use good judgment when deciding what to wear. Where you are going usually dictates what you wear.

Basic skill 8

Showing sensitivity to others

Everyone wants to be treated fairly. Hurting someone because he or she looks or acts differently is wrong. You become a better person when you help rather than hurt people. This is true in school, on a job, or at home. Showing sensitivity is a sign of maturity. It means that you recognize that everyone needs to be treated with kindness and understanding. Showing sensitivity to others means they're more likely to understand and respect your feelings.

Step 1. Express interest and concern for others, especially when they are having troubles.

Step 2. Recognize that disabled people deserve the same respect as anyone else.

Step 3. Apologize or make amends for hurting someone's feelings or causing harm.

Step 4. Recognize that people of different races, religions, and backgrounds deserve to be treated the same way as you would expect to be treated.

Showing sensitivity to others

Step 1. Express interest and concern for others, especially when they are having troubles.

Rationale:

If you help others, they are more likely to help you.

Helpful hints:

- If you see someone in trouble, ask if you can help.
- Sometimes, just showing you care is enough to help a person get through a difficult time.

Step 2. Recognize that disabled people deserve the same respect as anyone else.

Rationale:

A disability does not make a person inferior. Helping people with disabilities without ridiculing or patronizing them shows that you believe all people are equal, although some people need a little extra assistance.

Helpful hints:

- Be ready to help a disabled person when needed by doing such things as holding open a door, carrying a package, giving up your seat.
- Don't stare at disabled people or make comments about their special needs.

Step 3. Apologize or make amends for hurting someone's feelings or causing harm.

Rationale:

Saying you're sorry shows that you can take responsibility for your actions and can admit when you've done something wrong.

Helpful hints:

- You can harm someone by what you fail to do, just as easily as by what you do. Some examples are breaking a promise or not sticking up for someone who is being picked on.

- If you hurt someone, apologize immediately and sincerely.

Step 4. Recognize that people of different races, religions, and backgrounds deserve to be treated the same way as you would expect to be treated.

Rationale:

Treating others equally shows that although people are different, you believe that it shouldn't matter in the way you treat them.

Helpful hints:

- Don't make jokes and rude comments about the color of someone's skin or what he or she believes.

- Some people have different customs for doing things. Some people have more money than others. No matter, all people should be treated the same.

DATE DUE